Kinship

Poetry of

Changming Yuan

Goldfish Press
Seattle

Published by Goldfish Press, Seattle
2012 18th Avenue South
Seattle, WA 98144

Manufactured in the United States of America

ISBN 978-0978797560
Library of Congress Catalog Card Number 2015939851

Kinship

For Yuan Hongqi and Liu Yu
獻給我的父母親袁宏啟、劉瑜

By

Yuan Changming

Table of Contents

Your Dates: For Yuan Hongqi

Between
1934
And
2012
Is
A
Line
Short
But
Containing
Numerous
Dotted
Words

January 2: For Yuan Hongqi

That was the day when my father died
Before finishing the longevity noodles
Mom's trying to feed him below our feet
On the other face of the planet, where
He had persisted long enough to allow
Us to celebrate another new year's day
In Jingzhou as well as in Vancouver
When my brother's only son managed to
Travel all the way to Grandpa's dying bed
To report how he was doing in New York

This was also the time when I and Hengxiang
Felt like making love again after another
Cold war, when Iran successfully testfired
Two long-range missiles in the Persian Gulf
To deter the invasion to be led by Uncle Sam
And his running dogs, when the very first
Plymouth Neon was made in 2000, when JFK
Became a senator in 1960, when a stamped
Took 66 human lives after a soccer game
At the Ibrox Park Stadium in Scotland
Even earlier, and when God was taking
A long overdue nap, since he knew
All was well with this wild wild world

On that day, I became the oldest male
In my entire family, ready to take my turn
To deal with death in a masculine manner

Paper Plane: for Yuan Hongqi

I can never afford a spaceship
Nor do I even have a toy rocket
But I have many a sheet of paper
I have folded it, kept folding each

Into a plane, and launching it
From my humble homesite
One after another
High into the night sky

To fly close, closer, and the closest
To where his Buddhahood is sitting
Above a lotus flower, where his smile
Shines like the sunlight upon his sons

And grandsons down here, where he will catch
A plane gliding to him like a blue bird
Can you see its wings drafted with the poems
I have written for you, Dad

Private Talk: For Yuan Hongqi

Show yourself, Dad, I know you are around
Always trying like a true angel to protect
Me; let it be like those days when I was still
A teenager, but I will tell you all you wanted
To know about my feeling; for instance, I don't
Like you to force me to recite Chairman Mao's
Quotations, and I hope you would put Jin Yong
Rather than Karl Marx under my young pillow
Yes, let it be as if we were both younger, healthier
Suffering from no ischemia, our family curse
But having plenty of blood flowing behind our
Yellowish chests; let it be that we have no secrets
As father and son, and work together to help
Our offspring survive and succeed in this degrading
World, so full of snakes, snares and snobs

Inviting My Father's Spirit: For Yuan Hongqi

Never did we get along, Dad, before
You gave us all up, and seldom did
We even talk, so you had no idea of
How your son really felt about you
As a father, in particular, about your
Grooming habits: each time you
Returned from your office or trips
You skinned us off and washed all
Our clothes, sheets, towels, mops
Cleaning furniture (including
Every foot's bottom), polishing
Lamp covers and cooking utensils
Though you often forgot to put them
Back in good and tidy order; true
I learned to love your cleanness
But never the way you were so busy
Doing all this like an old woman

Now you are taking a long break
Up there, (where I supposed all
Is perfectly clean); do you, do
You enjoy watching me cleaning
Everything down here to keep
My home and heart dust-free?

A Memo: To Yuan Hongqi

Another thing I forgot to mention, Dad
Was I always believed you to be an
Extra-ordinary father, but in a highly
Embarrassing way: each time you saw
Me hanging around with my buddies
You kept saying this like a big broken
Gramophone: "Follow Chairman Mao's
Teachings; Follow the Party's great
Lead," just as you drove me crazy
By trying to convert me into a true
Communist like yourself, even
When we happened to be eating
At the same table. Still remember?
You once forced me to kneel down
On the hard ground until I finished
Reciting Mao Zedong's "Three Old
Essays." It was then I began to defy
You blindly, to follow no other than
My own heart, in a boyish rebellion
Against your fatherly dictatorship
Against any other form of tyranny

Walking with Father: For Yuan Hongqi

One thing I forgot to mention, Dad
Is I intentionally moved either before
Or behind you, each time we happened
To be walking together. That way, you could
Neither pinch my arm not slap my face
So readily; otherwise, you would have to
Embarrass yourself if you ran forward
Or waited to do so, as you tried to
Educate me in anger. Since my departure
From my home town beyond the pacific
How often have I hoped to walk again, just once
Side by side with you, getting or offering support
Whenever either of us needed it

But now I could only follow your footprints behind
Step by step, while you wait to beat me in heaven, smiling

Tomb Visiting: For Yuan Hongqi

Last year, before burying your ashes
Right beside Grandma's grave site
(To guard her Buddhaship, as you had
Wished), I opened your urn for a peek
And found your biggest bone chip
Glistening against the January wind
As pink as a piece of charcoal

Now, too far to attend your anniversary
Like every other good Confucian son
Burning joss sticks and fake money
Lighting a huge pile of firecrackers
Before your tombstone, on Big Wok Peak
But I did make three loud kowtows
Towards the east, and in so doing
I saw a little rosy cloud drifting around
Like an inflated bird beating its wings
Along the horizon, amid evening glows
And wondered whether that's your spirit
Still lingering between earth and heaven

What was it tightly holding in its beak:
A heirloom, or simply our family name?

[Although the poem was written early in 2012, it was round 10:30 pm on Saturday evening 30 December when my mom was conducting a traditional commemorating ritual in Jinzhou, China that I led my family actually to kowtow towards the east]

Recalling: For Yuan Hongqi

'Wait a while!' Mother would shout, 'they say
There might be more showers this afternoon.'
So I recalled, from time to time
How he would turn a deaf ear to her
And continue, dragging out quilts
Sheets, pillows, blankets, padded coats
One pile after another
Like moving forests
Hanging them on thick ropes
Tied to deformed poplars or lamp posts
'Not again! This old man of mine just wouldn't
Want to waste a single ray of sunlight.'
And remembered, for nearly half a century
My dad had tried each time to empty the whole house
And sun-wash everything, more like a grandma
Than like a father, even during the Cultural Revolution
Now realizing how I have been haunted
By his stark image, smiling, in blue, ever since
He nodded his head to Mother for the last time
About 5 pm on January 2 last year
I find myself choked again with gratitude:

It was my father who gave me so many a chance
To smell fresh sunlight in my boyish nightmares

Kinship: For Yuan Hongqi

Yes, we are father and son, but so often
Did I doubt this simple small biofact:
We could never say more than three short
Sentences to each other when we met, nor
Did we meet more than three times per year
Before I managed to flee a thousand miles
Away from you, and later ten thousand away
From your village on this world's other side

Like other Chinese fathers, you never said
You loved me, gave me a hug, or touched me
Unless it was a cutting pinch in the arm
Or a heavy hit on the butt, (always in surprise)
While my peers kept bragging aloud
About their great fathers, grandfathers
I looked down upon you, not because of
Your slight stature, but because of your
Smaller personality, constantly calling you
'A Buddha outside, a Devil at home'
(Of course behind your back), so I used to
Feel guilty, fearing I could never shed
Any teardrops when you die, just as every
True Confucian son is supposed to

Unlike me and my son, with a big store of
Co-memories ready to share, to cherish
We were born enemies, karma-determined
In our former lives, just as you had explained
To my mother, (who would be busy filling
In each new crack on our wall, with a big pail
Of muddy mixture every time we met)

Yet ever since your death at the dawn of 2012
I have been haunted by your image, kindly
Smiling, and even sobbed my heart out
While dreaming last night: are you there, Dad?

[This poem was nominated for the 2012 Pushcart Prize by *Mobius: the Poetry Magazine*]

Well, the Well: For Yuan Hongqi

In the lowest terrain of
My father's native village
Used to be an old well
As deep as the memories
Of last century, around which
Boys would be running
At noon in summer
And girls dancing under the willow
At midnight, where my father
Often sat, listening to his sick mother
Telling stories about his unknown ancestors

The well finally ran dry
After God knows how long, and
Since electricity came across the hills
And ponds, nobody has returned to it
Except mosses and lichens that have colonized
The whole territory, where only my grandma's ghost
Shines down from time to time
Trying to guard its walled-in secrets
Now as dry as its mouth

[This is a parallel poem based on an imagined experience.]

Ischemia: For Yuan Hongqi

In my line of people, especially on my father's side
There never seems to have been ample blood
Running within the arteries behind our Chinese chests
No matter how warm-hearted we actually are

As in the case of my father, who used to
Accuse me of being an ill-hearted teenager
My heart muscle is imbalanced
As one side is less infused with blood
Than the other, thus causing palpitation
Short breath, and a strong sense of
Tightness, heaviness or tiredness about life

To diagnose my cardiovascular defection
Neither an echo nor a stress test is needed
For I am keenly aware of my own doomed
Arteries that have been clotted
With too many syllables
Voiced or voiceless
And to make all these sounds flow out of my heart
Is already stressful enough
Nevertheless, I will keep pumping out these words
Be they ever so blood-soaked

[This is a parallel poem based on a puzzling health-related experience.]

Like A Lamp: For Yuan Hongqi

in Vancouver west
from time to time
you just cannot help yelling, yearning
for your father's humming
you fumble into musical halls
in pursuit of tunes
soft/hard utterances
you need this feeling
you need this contact
with origin
guiding your heart
like a lamp
along a forlorn road

[This is a parallel poem based on an imagined experience.]

Sowing after "Digging": For Yuan Hongqi

Above an empty sheet of paper
        With lines like the thin ridges
        In an open fallow field
My snug pen squats
        As if waiting in ambush
Below my window, my father's shaking shadow
        Is shrinking slowly but surely
        Into a focus constantly adjusted
                By the noon sun of spring
As he scatters some strange seeds
        Over the soil like salted brown rice
He has been preparing since last winter

By god, the old man enjoys sowing
        Even more than his old man

My grandfather died at the age of 29
        In a hilly village in central china
He had cast every drop of his soiled sweat
        Onto a field not belonging to himself
It is said that he reaped little in autumn
Nor did he really care about reaping

Like a bridegroom planting his plump sperm deep
        In his bride's virgin field on a mid-summer night
I am now sowing, with my pen

Making Tea: For Yuan Hongqi

Without a famous name
These little shy leaves
Coming afar from my father's farm
Deep among fluffy hills
Like sleeping giant pandas

Sowing a few in my crystal glass
I see them budding
Blooming in boiled water
Taking a slow sip
I fall drunk as if in a stupor
With a tiny taste of
All the freshness of spring
And a whole morning glow Making Tea

Without a famous name
These little shy leaves
Coming afar from my father's farm
Deep among fluffy hills
Like sleeping giant pandas

Sowing a few in my crystal glass
I see them budding
Blooming in boiled water
Taking a slow sip
I fall drunk as if in a stupor
With a tiny taste of
All the freshness of spring

[My father enjoyed drinking thick green tea, but this is a parallel poem based on an imagined experience.]

Sunwashing: For Yuan Hongqi

Never have I been a handy man
With my hands so too clumsy
Even to hold a hummer right
As my wife often jokes about them
But from my old man I did learn
How to make my home hygienic
By taking all bed clothing outside
On a good sunny Saturday
Opening all the doors and windows
To replace the abused air
Or even to remove the whole roof
If removable
So that my sons can dream
A sun-fresh dream at night
Just as I used to be so crazy
About the golden smell of sunlight

[My father would never waste a single ray of sunshine, as my mom often says: whenever it was sunny, he would put everything outside to enjoy some sunlight. I used to hate this addiction when I was a boy.]

Name Changing: For Yuan Hongqi

Confucius once said
If the name is not right
Language will carry no might
So my father created my name
By rearranging the sun and moon
Vertically and horizontally
To equip it with all
The forces of yin and yang
Dispersed in the universe

Since I became subject
To a totally different grammar
All people have complained
Or made fun of my name
So harsh and awkward
They conspire to seduce me
To adopt a familiar one
Like Michael in the powerful speech

But to retain the subtle balances
In the wild wild world I wander
To hold my father's sunbeam
With my mother's moonlight
I fiercely refuse to change it
Even though I often feel lost
When the sounds I hear
Do not sound like my name at all

The White Goose: For Yuan Hongqi

My grandfather was younger than my son
When he died of an undiagnosed disease
Somewhere in the Mid-South of China
So we have been told since childhood:
He did nothing memorable or forgettable
Left no picture of his or any handwriting
Not even one impression on my father's senses
Since he was born after he passed away)
But he had bought a big white goose
To protect his infant son in his place
And a single-syllabled family name
Copyrighting every little poem
I have composed
In a foreign tongue

Dusk Hanyang County: For Yuan Hongqi

Twilight Hanyang County
My father was eight
Yes, as young as eight
Maybe only seven
Burning with sweat
On his way to nowhere

In front of him a wild fellow dog
(He was a dog according to Chinese zodiac)
Was grumbling angrily with hanger
While dry grasses and leaves
Were swept from field to field
And rain clouds too heavy with dusk
Sacking down towards bald hills

Dying of thirst and heat
Both caused by an unknown fever
He dragged himself close to a pond
Smelling of rotten reeds and water buffalo shit
There he drank to his full
Wrapping his legs with fresh mud from the bottom
To keep himself cool for the night

The next morning he would continue
Wandering around outside his fatherless home
Like a premature vagrant

[When my father was orphaned at 13, he became a homeless boy travelling from Hanyang to Badong, Sichuan Province and then back to Shashi, Hubei Province, trying to find a job to make a living until 1949.]

A Dream Or a Metaphor?: A Fatherly Soliloquy

The other night, before the cock crowed, or
The crow cocked out of darkness, a yellowish
Shape stalked my vision, as in blank verse,
"Mark me," it said, sounding almost exactly
Like my late father: "Take very serious heed,
Hearing what I shall unfold." Suddenly alerted,
I got up among others between dream and sleep.
"When you were a teenager, I hated you so much
For looking at me always with those sideways eyes,
Giving me an ugly face each time I talked to you,
So much so that I cursed you numerous times in
My dreams for being such an unworthy son; I often
Doubted if you were my own flesh, until you grew
Into a normal, loving adult, making me feel guilty
For life; I was even suspicious of your mother
Betraying me, not only in heart but also in body;
I almost caught her making love with some guy
On our own bed. You still remember that small
Apartment we used to live in? Among all my deadly
Secrets, these two I want to reveal to you first.
Next time, I will tell you more about the limbo
Between hell and heaven, the slightest word about
Which may harrow the spirit, or burn the blood.
But, alas, now the cock crows, and I must vanish.

Just Another Rainy Day: For Liu Yu

It rains a lot in Vancouver
Often does this rain remind me of
The days when you sojourned here
With my family, after Father left all of us

While walking in the rain, you would
Recall, under my big umbrella
How you once awaited in a drizzle
With me in a broken basket on your back
To cross the widening river, not far
From our village when I was crying hard
For a large spoonful of flour soup (you were too
Weak and too hungry to produce any milk)
Seeing you do nothing about my hunger
The ferry man asked, *Where is its mom?*
I am his mother! You replied, hot tears rolling down
With the cold raindrops on your childish face
How old are you then? – Almost 17.

It is now raining again in Vancouver, and beyond this rain
Your voice echos aloud on the other side of this world

Seasonal Greetings: For Liu Yu

Rather than composing poetry
To commemorate you after you are gone
I am now writing, dear Mom
To pay my highest tribute to you
As one of the hardest-fated on earth

Yes, among the many death experiences you've had
The most significant one for me (and my sons)
Was your sickness you suffered at two, which was so
Severe that your poor and ignorant foster mother
Could do nothing but put you on a flat basket
And return your living corpse to your bio-creator

But for your step father, who used his shamanic skills
To contain the evil spirit and drive it to an unknown
Corner, you would have died like a doomed sapling
(That's why your name is changed to 'Refound')

So, stay well, Mom, and remain hardy for us!

Never Too Late to Learn: For Liu Yu

Hi, Mom, how are you doing this couple of days?

Last night, I told my younger son how you used to be
The best student in your village school, how you won
A scholarship to attend junior high school, but failed
To go because you did not have the one dollar enough
To eat for a whole month. He really felt sorry for you
And fortunate for himself. Yes, because of your very
Dreams about school, you have a son with a PhD
In Canada, a grandson with a PhD from NYU…
Remember? It is you who taught your ageing son
To use an iPad to buy and sell high-tech stocks
The other day, and I found it really amazing, not about
My own reluctance to learn anything new, but about
Your readiness to experiment with your mind and
Fingers, both of which are now almost 80 years old

This Is A Line: For Liu Yu

A line this is for my mother's birthday
A birth line for my mother's day
A mother for the birthday of a line
A celebration of my mother's line of birth

Mother, I will line your birth with celebration
I will day a line with birth celebration, Mother
I will mother a day line with celebration
I will celebrate the mothering of a line
Mother, I will celebrate a line's birthday

Mother my celebration of a line's day
Mother my day's line for a birthday
Celebrate my line with my mother's birth
Celebrate the day with my mother's line
Mother, I celebrate your birthday with a line

Twilight: For Liu Yu

My heart muscle contracts, excruciatingly
Like an overly-wound spring, ready to break
Each time I imagine my mom walking alone
Towards the dusty evening, while she used to
Go downstairs first, waiting aloud for my dad:
'Grandpa, what are you still busy doing there?
It's time to take a walk outside, along the moat!'

Now without a companion, my mother does not
Have to wait or hurry for anyone, but how she
Just misses the days when her shadow and my
Father's became longer and longer, side by side
As they strolled slowly, until the sun set lower
And lower above the blurred horizon of autumn

In-Carnations: For Liu Yu

Like broken pieces
Of charcoal, glistening
Against spring cold
These pink petals
Are not tears you
Shed over my death
Rather, they are
Incarnations of
God and Devil
Blooming in blood
Out of my heart
But do not feel sad, Mother

On the Mother's Day: For Liu Yu

This is the very first and last time
We celebrate a non-Chinese holiday
Here in a chosen country
At a chosen time: Today, I have had
A chance to treat my mom (visiting us
From the other side of the world
After my dad's death) to a dinner
At Southsea Fish Village, where she tasted
Dishes like abalone and shark fin soup
Finally affordable, all freshly served
Out of my poetry, before my poet son
Cut my wife a single lilac flower
From the front yard of his teenager heart

Mahjong Marching: For Liu Yu

When a crow chats with another crow intimately, or a dog writes poetry on my frosted lawn, can we still see ourselves as humans capable of 'modern behaviour'?

hongzhong (Red Middle)

While my mind tries to find a way
Out of the labyrinth
Walled with thick wishes
My body is left behind, wandering
Like a headless fly flying around
In a vast desert, another labyrinth, unwalled

facai (Prosperity)

As the whole world keeps running amuck
in its thin and pale dreams drifting like mists
I stand still, watching in dark stillness
Afraid to awake and shock
All the dreamers at midnight
To a shameful death

baiban (Whilte Board)

Since my parents hurriedly
Put this yellowish ticket into my hand
I have been trying, trying really hard
To catch the right bus
Running fast somewhere
Before it expires shortly

Farewell Talk: For Liu Yu and Yuan Hongqi

Well… Old Liu, I have said all
That I have …to say, just as I've done
All that I can …do

Sure, Old Man, so you can die
A happy death now, and I will
Follow to accompany you shortly

What a comfort! We have two …filial sons
To …outlive us, and three great grandsons
To carry our …bloodline on

Indeed, they bring true honor to the family
Name: one is a pioneering engineer
In Silicon Valley, another is doing his PhD
In New York, and the youngest has published
A poetry book in Vancouver though still a teenager

But both of us …grew up in poor Chinese villages
You …barely finished your elementary school
While I had only two …years of education

Really, this contrast alone makes us all happy
And proud enough, just as our elder son called
To stress this from Canada yesterday evening

Well, fare…well, I am going first; once… I find the
Way to the Pureland, I will …return to take you…

But don't be in such a hurry yet, Old Man
For I wish to take care of our two ageing sons
For a few more years. Hey, *nihao* Nurse

Triple Tribute: To Yuan Hongqi and Liu Yu

In this entire world, I am now
The only one who truly knows
You are still alive. You see

As part of you, I have grown
Talented enough to represent your
Most memorable pasts without
Having to carving them on a
High-standing marble tombstone

Also, I have become rich enough
To keep all your genetic records
In the safest safe within my plain
Mind instead of a fancy cyberstation

More important, I have turned strong
Enough to uphold your spirit firmly
In my body and carry it forward
Until it blooms among my off-spring

Yes, in this little poem, I, for one, know
You are still as much alive as these words

Parcenary: For Yuan Hongqi and Liu Yu

my destination was preset
you will receive a parcel
by express. It turns out

all too expressly, and
the sender was my parents
who had wrapped themselves
inside already

Reading behind the Lines: For Yuan Hongqi and Liu Yu

Behind the words is there no meaning squatting
Except a bold row of cheerful cherry trees
Standing tall in front of my half-fenced house
That bloom for two weeks in a year only
Between spring and summer

Behind the words is there no emotion hidden
But a pair of little unsung yellow birds
Popping up from nowhere
One has flown far away from home
The other still learning to fly close to the nest

Behind the words is there no metaphor explored
But a black and white photo of my parents
Who are hospitalized alternately in China
For the imbalance between yin and yang
A disease both blood-related

Ancestry Worshipping: For Yuan Xizheng

No, we never planned it that way
But it so happened this seventh summer
I took my twelve-year-young son
To my father's native village among hairless hills
In the far east end, the other side of the world
Which he had left as a starving orphan
And returned with me in the Mao suit
Like a magic-toyed boomerang
When we were both at Allen's age
For the first times in our lives

Last time, my father forced the Little Red Guard in me
To kowtow, burn joss sticks and paper money secretly
For his parents, whose dialect had survived
Though I understood it only half-heartedly

This time, I cajoled my boy to grasp a handful of earth
From the grave of my grandma worshipped by villagers
(Her humaneness has supposedly made her a local deity)
And smuggle it to the backyard of our home in Vancouver
Like some foreign seeds prohibited at the customs

As we departed, again, our clan elder chanted:
Under the shade of a new highway
This old grave will soon be erased...

The Death of a Chinese Widow: For Li Juying

In a remote Chinese village
On a forgotten winter night
A 38-year-old poor woman
Tried hard to sit up noiselessly
Put aside rather than on her padded clothes
Crawled out of her frameless bed
And resolutely drowned herself
In a broken wide-brimmed water jug

Behind herself she left neither worth nor words
Except three teenagers who had been
Bullied and looked at with slanting white eyes
By their fellow villagers
(who bore the same family name)
Ever since their father died
Of an untreated disease
13 years before

Years later, her children understood
Why she killed herself
In a water jug on that night
Many years after she had been suffering
From a painful
But not fatal disease

Years later, her only son told me
Why my grandma
Chose to drown herself almost naked
On that cold night

[My father was choked with tears every time he said he was never able to perform a son's loving duty, since his mother committed suicide to save family resources when he was only 13 years old. So, he insisted in having some of his ashes divided to be buried beside her tomb to do so. We honoured this wish of his, and to express my feeling, I wrote the above poem to commemorate my grandma.]

Four Masculine Haiku: A Poetic Family

Debao
Head and heart both bald
He's not pulled out one single line
Except his surname

George
Using no poet's lathe
He shaves off his young manhood
With an e-razor

Allen
Like son, like father
His voice has begun to break
All for poetry's sake

Michael
To his great credit
He's published two finest sons
Among his fine poems

Curse in Verse: An Ischemic Tradition*

As if this had been a family curse
You have all the symptoms of ischemia:
Palpitations, short breaths, irregular heartbeats
Although no test results show you
Having a physiological cause of the problem

While your family doctor keeps wondering
Why you do not have enough blood
Flowing around behind your Chinese chest
You know your heart muscle as a sponge
From which you have squeezed out
Too many of your blood-rooted words
Like your father, like your son

[While my dying father Yuan Hongqi has never been able to get his poetry published, my 16-year-old younger son Allen Qing Yuan, who suffers greatly from disc problems, has already had his poems appearing in a number of countries.]

Family Reunion: Once and Forever

Yuan Hongqi, may your spirit, Dad, come
And join us from Pure Land in this poem
(Conceived in and dedecated to Vancouver)
With Liu Yu, my mother, who is paying us
A visit from the other side of the world
Let's gather together behind these thin lines
Where I and Hengxiang Liao, my old girl
Have prepared a big dinner according to
Our own recipes. Please, sit here with Mom
Above my central metaphor. First, take a sip
Of Luosong Soup, our only family specialty
George Lai and Allen Qing, my two sons
Always love to drink, even Hyunjung Lee
(George's Korean wife) finds it agreeable --
By the way, the young couple has finally
Decided to buy a condominium in Sunnydale
Now, try some consonance, and this assonance
Fried with Tofu, a course you never heard of
In your lifetime. Look, right beside you is
Julian Han Yuan, your most favored grandson
The pride of our family who's doing his PhD
In New York, and across the table are Liu Yun
My brother and his current wife Chen Jing
Still working far away in Jingzhou, China

Dad, since you were a vegetarian, a Buddhist
Let's have internal rhyme instead of wine, let's
Celebrate our grand family reunion. Cheers!

[Towards the end of 2011, we had our first and last family gathering when my father was still alive. In terms of health and finance, this was a highly costly reunion, as George and Hyunjung had to travel from San Francisco, Julian from New York, and we - my wife, my younger and i, from Vancouver all the way to Jinzhou in Hubei Province. Because of this trip, Allen's disc problem got worse and has never recovered, while I began to suffer from dramatically obvious symptoms of heart diseases such as HCM (?)]

Etc.

we, yuan ii, by the grace
of god, emperor and autocrat of
all english words, king of dreamland
grand duke of assonance and
consonance, author of
allen qing yuan, architect of
george lai yuan, last scribbler of
poetic lines, et cetera et cetera
et cetera et cetera etc

herein proclaim ourselves as no extra ordinary line
but an ellipsis...

Entering Adulthood: To George and Allen

The most important tip for you, Sons
Is to forget all the tips any father
Any book, any computer can give you
About this world, but just remember
This: the moment you step
Out of the boundary of our little home
You will have to remain
On high alert, even while dreaming
What you will cross is a snakeland, where
There is as much sunshine, fresh air
As many blue skies, green leaves
Fragrant flowers, handsome
Human figures, as cobras, mambas
Taipans, adders, kraits and vipers

Song of a Tone-Deaf: for Allen and George Yuan

There is often such a time when you, a no-songster
Would want to sing aloud to yourself, a song
That everyone else might also love to sing; the song
Whose lines you never remember, nor can you
Control your pitch as it rises and falls randomly
On its own, nor will you keep the tune on the
Right track; the song whose rhythm you do not
Care to follow, while lost in your little privacy
The song that has an evasive melody
Deeply encoded in your heart

Although you sound like a duck or donkey
Your voice is full of euphonies

Knitted Vest: For George Lai Yuan

son, this is not a fancy
or fashionable garment
but a deep rooted gift
for your first departure from home
from your foreign grandma
quite alive beneath your feet
on the other side of earth
who you know neither speaks
your adopting language
nor wants to write you anything
that needs to be translated
but she has hand-knitted
needle after needle
needle after needle
with vegetable-dyed wool
all she means to say to you
(at the aged shiny kitchen table
in the middle of a rice field
on the bank of the yangtse river
or below the yellowish family album)
into this simple and solid clothe
which she tells me to retell
will support your bare back
during your flight in the sky
warm your homesick heart
between cold sights of strangers
against the heavy daily loads
just like the worn-out one
i am still wearing even today
as her little ageing boy
who has traveled thus far

Man’s Mutation: For George

dear god, i often wonder
in bitter sweetness
or sweet bitterness
whether i or my first home computer
is the real father of my son
who i well remember
was not conceived in a chip
but seemed to have been delivered
at the wrong website
breastfed at chat rooms
brought up in a silver cyber space
as he just refuses to grow
into a full human being
like myself, my father
or my father's father
i know he is not really a monster
but only a cold blooded hybrid
between my high mind and high tech
so forever lost in virtual reality
that no birth day celebrations
are loud enough to wake him up
from his quasi hibernation
on the little mouse pad

Fatherly Fear: For Allen Qing Yuan

how much
just how much love should I show you, Son
I do not know, I only know
how I had tried
how I'd persisted in having you as my second child, a lifelong companion to your bro
how I had found the greatest joy in merely seeing you after each long and hard day
but I never meant for you to have been
36 days prematurely born, and to have begun
Suffering so much when you were only 12 years old, suffering
from a terrible drought within your Chinese skin, suffering
from bulged disks that cause you to walk like a cripple, suffering
from sciatic pain when you move around, suffering
from having to withdraw from your school's volleyball team, suffering
from lacking the confidence to emulate your elder brother, suffering
from your limitations to kick, jump, run, bend like your friends, suffering
from your inability to work outside home to earn your own money, oh Son
I do not know, I do not know how much love I should show to you:
if a bit too little, you would feel disappointed of my fatherly love
if a bit too much, I fear heavens would be so jealous as to take you away from me

indeed, how much
just how much love should I show you, Son
I do not know, I only know
after I die, my other self will stand right behind your back
wherever you are, whenever there is or there is no sunshine
ready to protect you against all evil gods and ghosts

but while still alive, I do not know, Son
how much love I should show you:
if a bit too little, you might feel disappointed of my fatherly love
if a bit too much, I fear heavens might be so jealous as to take you away from me

Allenian Dragonmania

my younger son is the greatest fun
    of dragons i've ever known as a chinaman
he could lecture hours nonstop
    on their various magic talents
not knowing they are devilish
    beyond the touch of his mother tongue
he often insists in his own room
    everything is transformed from a dragon
once he asked me in loud indignation
    why he was not born in the year of dragon

on a white night with a black fright
allen shrieked all his way to my dream
    confused, confounded and horrified
    till he told me a fantastic tale:
a real living dragon in its proto form
    had thrown a visit through his window
    confessing behind his mind's curtain
it had been deeply touched
    by the tremendous tenders of affection
    my son had made to him in private

When Burying Me: For Allen Qing Yuan

First, remove all my clothes and masks
That I have been tired of wearing, skinned off
The tattoos on my chest, my heart, my soul

I have kept as my secrets. Then send me
Into the resomator like an alchemist, with the
Words I have used most often, the images

I have created and collected in my mind
Burn me as the Dao God did the Monkey King
With the purest fire from hell, from heaven

Tongues of blue gas, or red electricity
Sizzling, I will enjoy being kissed first and
Last, by my own words, my own metaphors

September 7: For AQY

The other night, I dreamed I carried my teenager
Son in a big brown-colored paper bag under my
Left arm, trying to plod my way to the hospital
In the rain in a strange town; as I trudged forward
I found him somehow shrinking into two femurs
And vanishing into the sky, like the yellow crane
In a legend of my native land. In grief, I cried my
Heart out, until I saw him returning to my mom's
Mud-floored, straw-thatched home, big and strong
Smiling in his boyish face. Suddenly thrown into
Such ecstasy, I could not help kneeling down, kow-
Towing to him as if he were my Buddhist master
When I told my mother the next day, she laughed
Aloud on the world's other side: it was good omen
Meaning our Allen Is going to survive and succeed

Codicil: To Allen Qing Yuan

After I die, Son
Wrap my body with my poems
Put all my remains
In an e.cask, and send it
To a site that will
Never be on hiatus

By burying me online
You can readily
Trace my soul traveling
From one living screen
To another
As long as you have access
To the virtual space

Note: To Allen

feel happy for me
when i die, son
i will have finally waked from
    a long and heavy dream
beginning to travel
    with all leisure and pleasure
in a far lighter and brighter place
    like a shapeless shadow on this earth
        to guide and safeguard you
            my ever truer self

At the Kitslano Beach: For Allen

i spot and pick up
    a curious clam
whose flimsy lips fairly open
    and her tongue keeps reaching out
    as if to reveal
  the saltiness of seawater
  the sad face of sand
  and anecdotes about certain fishes
whose narration i really do not understand
    although my younger son assures me
he can

Inner Drought*: For Allen Yuan

In this lower mainland, rain is the order
Of the day: while the drizzle moisturizes
Dreams and drama alike, storms have filled
Every crack and crevice with seasonal juice

But deep in your body has been a drought
Persisting ever since your birth, no plant
Grows green enough, no bird comes to perch
On a bough, all pipes and rivulets dry

Oh, for a rich rain to moisten and irrigate your
Inner fields, your cells, your nerves, your hopes
I would sacrifice my fatherhood, provided you
Could take a shower in the open, with your spine
Stemming straight like a strong young tree

*My 15- year-old son Allen has had a disc problem since 2008, which has resulted, according to traditional Chinese medicine, from the internal 'dryness' he was born with.

Growing Up: For Big Al

soon after his fifth birthday
my little allen solemnly promised
to purchase someday
    a huge house for mom
    a big benz for dad
    a mighty motorcycle for bro
    and a big pail of paint for grandpa

two birthday cakes before
he often imitated
    playing "wild wild west"
    with a broken broom
        as his electric guitar
    and when he was a second grader
he asked me many times
    whether he could make big bucks
    by becoming a street musician

now he has just blown out his ten candles
    finally begun to learn playing guitar
    whose sounds he finds really fascinating
although he still cannot keep the right beats
    with neither his simple music
    nor his feeling about future
    nor his past pledges
he is trying hard to play
    his the song of his own choice

Allen in Wonderland

Qucheng
Homerburgh
Dantefield
Shakespeareston
Goethestadt
Pushkingrad
Baudelaireville
Nerudastad
Frostdale
Tagorerboro

Picking Blueberries in Richmond: For AQY

on a summer afternoon
i take my little allen
far to a field near the forest
of some cheerful cherry trees
where he could jump wildly
on ever-naked soil
finger the freshness of fruit
and smell the scarlet of nature
letting the wanton wind
blow hard and straight
through his limbs and senses
long numbed in the city pen
by the heavy grey of cement
it is really fun, dad
and the cherries are so delicious
yes, but the trees are hard to grow, son

Sleeping in the Same Room: For Liu Yun

how fortunate I am
to be your brother
(only occasionally visiting you
from the other side of our planet)
rather than your wife: I can never
stand your snorting
not because I would have to
choke myself constantly with insomnia
but because I would be worried to death
about the way you might stop breathing
while we are still dream-chatting
about how we were often deeply trapped
in the frog pond
of our naked boyhoods

Husbandly Hope: For HL

Whether made of bamboo or ivory
They are a pair of Chinese chopsticks
That have to function together every time
To taste the dishes put on the dinner table

Getting Newly Old: For Helen Liao

you can only talk
about what you used to do
and do
what you used to talk about

you shrink in both ways
and both ways are
the only way
to shrink

what's supposed to be hard
softens like a boiled noodle
what's supposed to be tender
hardens like a winter stone

one attempt
on top of another

or, one attemptable night
after another

Domestic Democracy: For a Baby Wife

She is always in perfect health
Except she is super-allergic to criticism
Indeed, even a suggestion about a small error
Would cause her to resent against you for a whole month
If you say this dish tastes a bit too salty
She would yell: "From now on, you do the cooking!"
When you advise her not to buy junk food for your teenager son
She would buy more for the months to come
After you hint that she might have written another wrong check
She would refuse to make love for an entire season
Before you attempt to have a nice chat with her
She would make a sarcastic remark
That she has been refining since last year
So you keep communication at the minimum level
Just to maintain normal family functions
Until you two feel too happy to continue the cold war
About how much more assets you have newly accumulated

Never make any negative hints about your woman
Or you will be drowned to a slow death in this swirling cycle

Simple Natural Labour Division: For HL

She shops for every piece of grocery
    I pay every small or big bill
She does all the cooking
    I wash dishes, most of the time
She cleans all the surfaces
    I put all items in proper places
She washes everyone's clothes with a machine
    I pull out every weed with my hands
She makes sure all doors are locked at night
    I make bed every morning
She takes out garbage once a week
    I sunbathe quilts and blankets once a month
She files a major complaint every season
    I file our tax returns every year
She does everything else against her habit
    I do all other stuffs according to my interest

A New Recipe She Invents after 25 years of Marriage: For Helen

'yummy, it tastes so good!' he exclaimed.

'really?' she asked.

'where did you learn the recipe?
These steamed fish chips are really delicious
With all this shredded green onion and fresh ginger.'

'well, this is the third time I cooked
it this way. Do you really mean
you like the dish?'

'of cuz! Why would I want to lie
about the food YOU cook?'

'well, this is the only thing
i am never sure about you.'

'are you?!'

H: For Hengxiang Liao

inspired by a fence in hell
you were invented long ago
to connect every human
for a tall ladder of hope
that we can stand high
against the blue horizon
like the Babel Tower growing to reach Him
where I can find a home in the fame hall
where I can settle my soul in heaven

Fare-Well, Darling: To H

On that evening, as our titanic
Finally began to sink, how I desperately
Combed our whole boat
To find you the only lifebuoy aboard!
But when I returned empty-handed
I saw you struggling fiercely
In the water of cold night
Already far beyond my reach
[With the ring hidden beside your arm]

Last Words to HL

As always, I am really very very sorry, darling
For all that you have had to go through simply
To remain my wife. While I love you, treasure
You, you have seldom cared about me, especially
Since we got married. Indeed, you have been trying
Very hard to be a reasonably dutiful spouse, yet
You never touch me, respect me, but treat me no more
Or no less than a money-making machine, ready
To leave me when you find me hopelessly too poor
Making love from time to time with someone else
Right in the kitchen of your heart, I know all that

I know all this has been very hard for you, darling
But now you are becoming truly free, free from me
Free from any restrictions, Chinese or foreign, you
Can do whatever you want with your heart or body
To pursue your girlish romanticism or fantasies
The moment I breathe out this last syllable of mine

Be well, darling, I know you will forget me soon and
Have many more years to live. And I am sorry, darling
Really, I am deeply sorry to have kept you for so long

Acknowledgements

First and foremost, my deepest gratitude to my publisher Mr Koon Woon, without whose editorial expertise, friendly encouragement and artistic devotion this chapbook would never have become a physical reality.

Moreover, I would like to take this opportunity to mention all the literary outlets that have encouraged me as an author since I began to publish poetry in English in mid-2005. As a matter of fact, most of the poems included in this collection have appeared in at least one of the following:

In print:
Australia: *dotdotdash, LiNQ, Windmills*
Austria: *Poetry Salzburg Review*
Canada: *All Rights Reserved, Alone Together* (anthology), *ARC, Ars Medica, Best Canadian Poetry* (2009;12;14; Anthology), *Canadian Literature, Carte Blanche, CV2, the Dalhousie Review, dANDelion, Descant, Divine Intimacy* (Anthology), *Earls Court, English 113 F1* (Courseware, Univ. of Alberta), *Estuary, Event, Existere, Feathertale Review, filling Station, Freefall, Grain, Jones Av, Literary Review of Canada, Marriage* (Anthology), *Matrix, the Nashwaak Review, the New Chief Tongue, the New Quarterly, NoD, One Cool Word, Other Voices, Ottawa Arts Review, Overseas Chinese Poetry (Chinese), Poetry Canada, Polychrome Ink, the Prairie Journal, Queen's Quarterly, Quills Canada Poetry Magazine, Qwerty, Rampike, A Rewarding Life* (anthology), *Ricepaper, Rhubarb, Spirituality* (Anthology), *Wascana Review, Windsor Review, Vallum, Vancouver Review*
Cyprus: *Sons of Camus Writers International Journal*
China: *Asia Literary Review (hk), World Poetry Yearbook 2014, Yuan Yang(hk)*
Egypt: *Rowayat*
Germany: *SAND Journal*
India: *MetVerse Muse, Prosopisia, Reading Hour, Taj Mahal Review*
Ireland: *Boyne Berries*
Israel: *Voice Israel*
Italy: *Private: International Review of Black and White Photographs and Texts*
Japan: *Ginyu, Poetry Kanto*
Norway: *Two Thirds North*
Romania: *Acolada & Confesiun (anthology), Actis Lidia, Contemporary Literary Horizon, haiku anthology, Egphobia,*
South Africa: *New Coin*
Thailand: *Destroyer of worlds (anthology), From When and Where (co-authored)*
Turkey: *Istanbul Review*
UK: *Aligater Stew, Animal Antics*(Anthology), *Atlantean, Breadline, Brittle Star, Cadenza, Cannon's Mouth, Confingo, Current Accounts, Decanto, First Time, Decanto, Forward Press (*Anthology, *2009, 2010, 2011), Gold Dust, Horrified Press* (Anthologies: housewife +end], *the Journal, the London Magazine, the New Writer, Orbis, Parameter, Pennine Ink, Poetic Hours, Polluto, PostPoetry, Pulsar, Sein und Werden, Sufi, Transnational, Turbulence, Visionary Tongue, Voice of the Bard* (Anthology), *Wasafiri, World Strand* (Anthology)
US: 3rd Wednesday, *580 Split, Abandoned Towers, After Hours, Ampersand Review, Aries, Anthology of Best Present Day Poems, Baltimore Review, Barrow Street, Berkeley Poetry Review,* BILiNE (anthology), *Birmingham Arts Journal, Black Magnolias Lit J, Blinking Cursor, Byline, Burning Word, Cake Magazine, Calliope, Chaffey review, the Chaffin Journal, CHEST, Chrysanthemum, Cider Press Review, Circles Show, Cirque, Clare, Controlled Burn, Crosstimbers, Delmarva Review, Dirtcakes* (Anthology), *El Portal, Ellipsis, Emerge Literary Journal, Encyclopedia Project (v.3), Evening Street Review, Fact-Simile, Fairy Tale Review, FEILE-FESTA, Flower & Vortexes, Foundling Review, FreeFall, Fresh!* (Anthology), *Grace Notes Magazine, Grey Sparrow, Gris Gris, Haarp, Hawaii Review, Hidden Oak, Homestead Review, I-70 Review, Idiom, IF Poetry Journal, Impeachable, In Our Own Words* (Anthology), *Inkspill,*

Instigatorzine, International Poetry Review, Iodine Poetry Journal, Ivy (Chinese), James Dickey Review, KNOCK, Labletter, Left Curve, Literary Mary Journal, Literature Today; the Lost Country, the Mas Tequilas Review, Meadow, Midwest Quarterly, Moon City Review, Mobius,Nebo, New Binary Press (Anthology), *Nibble, Nomad's Choir, the Northridge Review, the Other Herald, Out of Our, Overplay/Underdone* (Anthology), *Owen Mister Review, pacificREVIEW, Palehouse, Penny Ante Feud, Perceptions, Perspectives (anthology), Petals in the Pan (anthology), Phantom Drift (anthology), Phati'tude, Pinyon Review, Poe Little Thing, Poesia, Poetalk, Poetry for the Masses, Pom-Pom-Pomeranian, Porcupine Literary Arts Magazine, Porter Gulch Review, Portland Review, Prime Mincer, PRISM Review, Progressive Poetics, Prospectus, Pudding Magazine, Rabbit Catastrophe Review, Raven Chronicles, Red Rock Review, Redactions, Relief* (Anthology), *Remark, , RHINO, RipRap, Rockford Review, Rockhurst Review, Rune, Rhythm + PUNishment, Salamander, San Clara Review, Saranac Review, Schuylkill Valley Journal, Sentence: A Journal of Prose Poetics, Segue, Sephyrus Press Afterlife* (Anthology), *Shalla Magazine, Side B, Sierra Nevada Review, Solo Novo, SP Quill, Spillway, Spirits, Straylight, Stealing Time, Still Crazy, Stoneboat Review, Studio 1, Sugar House Review, Tales of Talisman, Taproot Magazine, Threepenny Review, Time of Singing, Tipton Poetry Journal, Tule Review, Ucity Review, Urthona, US-China Review, Vehicle, Vermilion Literary Project, Verse/Chorus (anthology), Waterhshed, Waterways, Weber Review, Westward Quarterly, Willard & Maple, Wordgathhering, World Literary Today, Write On, Writing for Peace, Words & Images, You Are Here*

Online :
Australia: foam:e, *Mascara literary Review, Otoliths, Peril, Snorkel, Stylus Poetry Journal, Structo*
Bulgaria: *Public Republic*
Canada: *Apollo's Lyre, Ascent Aspirations Magazine, Autumn Leaves, Branch, Bywords, Centrifugal Eye, Estuary, Fieldstone Review, Hart House Review, Inscribed, Maynard, Egregious, MTLS, Northern Cardinal Review, Other C/lutter, Poetry in Voice (online anthology), Poetry Pacific, Rhythm, Toronto Quarterly, Writers Block, Ygdrasil, Zouch;*
China (Hong Kong): *Cha, Balloons Literary Journal, Far Enough East*
Finland: *Nokturno*
France: *Belleville Park Pages, Paris/Atlantic*
Germany: *Chrysanthemum*
India: *Atlas Poetica, Brown Criticque, Contemporary Literary Review: India, Creativica, Criterion, Earthen Lamp, Enchanted Verse Literary Review, the Four Quarters Magazine,* Galacy: Int'l Multidiscplinary Reseach, *Guwahatian, Indian Rev, Kritya, Lakeview International Journal of Literature and Arts, Muse India, New Aesthetic, Open Road Review, Outside In, Sangam, Thanal*
Ireland: *A Ulster, Silver Apple,*
Italy: *Gi amici di Guido Gozzano, Immagina & Poesia, Private online*
Japan: *Asahi Shimbun*
Kenya: *Kwani?*
Malaysia: *Anak Sastra, Malaysia Poetic Chronicles*
Mexico: *In Other Words*
Nepal: *The Applicant*
New Zealand: *Numinous, Rem, Southern Ocean Review*
Nigeria: *Saraba Magazine*
Philippines: *Electronic Maroon*
Romania: *Nazar Look*
Singapore: *Quarterly Literary Review of Singapore*
Sweden: *Mediterranean Poetry*
Thailand: *Aaron, Eastlit*
Turkey: *Istanbul Literary Review*
UAE: *Sukoon*
UK: *7th Quarry Poetry Magazine, 20X20, Allegro Poetry Magazein, Argotist, Conversation Papers, Counter Culture, Dawntreader, Dark Fiction Spotlight, Delinquent, Electric Eel, Erbacce, Horror Zine, Glasgow Review, Greatworks, Gulper Eel, Ink Sweat & Tears, Interpoetry, mgversion2>datura, Nib, Nthposition, Onedit, Outlaw Poetry Network, Parameter, the Poetry Box (Horror and Dark P M); Poetry Kit, Poetry Scotland, Screech Owl, Stub, Talking Verse, Three and a Half Point 9, Twisted Tongue, Winamop*

US: *4 & 20, 6 Little Things, 13 Myna Bird, 322 Magazine, 1st Bird Review, 34 Parallel, 40 Ounce Bachelor, 322 Review, Aaduna, About Place, Ad Astra. Agave, Aji Mag, Altered Scale, Amulet, Analogpress, And/Or, Anemone Sidecar, Apropos Literary Journal, A River and Sound Review, A Shot of Ink, Aries, Assisi, Alba, Alehouse, Alliterati, Amaranthine Muses, Amarillo Bay, Anemone Sidecar, Apocryphal Text, Apparatus, Aroostook Review, Asia Writes, Asinine, Askew Poetry, Artistic Muse, Assonance, Atlas and Alice, Avalon Lit Rev, Avatar Review, Avocet Review, Awosting Alchemy, Backlit Barbell, Bad Futurist, Bangalore Review, Bare Hands, Barefeet Review, Barely South Review, Barnwood Poetry Magazine, the Bat Shat, Belle Reve, Bibliotheca Alexandrina, Bicycle Review, Big Pulp, Big River Poetry Review, Bijou Poetry Review, Binnacle, Birds we pile loosely, Bird's Eye Review, the Bitchin' Kitsch, Black Fox Lit Mag, Black Heart Magazine, Black Magnolias, Black Petals, Black Wire Literary Magazine, Blackdahlia, BlazeVox, the Bleeding Lion, Blood Lotus Journal, Blood Moon Rising Mag, Blue Bonnet Review, Blue Fifth Review, Blue Heron Rev, the Blue Hour, Blue Lake Review, Blue Lyra Review, Blue Moon Lit & Art Review, Blue Print Review, Bluepepper, Bluestem, The Body Attacks Itself, Booth, Breath & Shadow, the Boiler Journal, Brink Magazine, Broad, Bicl Pff. Buddhist Poetry Review, Bumples, Burst, Cactus Heart, A Capella Zoo, Calliope Nerve, Camel Saloon, Canyon Voices, Caper, Carcinogenic Poetry, Cardinal Sins, Cascadia Review, Cave Moon, Cell 2 Soul, Chantarelles Notebook, Chaparral, Christian Living in the Mature Years, Children, Chrysalis, Churches & Daddies, Cincinnati Review, Circle Review, Clutching at Straw, Cliterature, Clockwise Cat, Clover, Coachella Review, Coffee Shop Poems, Coffeine Destiny, Commonline, Concelebratory Shoehorn Review, Composite, Congruent Spaces Magazine, Connotation, Construction, the Copperfield Review, the Cortland Review, Counterexamples Poetics, CounterPunch, Crab Fat Mag, Crack the Spine, Crazy Concrete, Crash, Cricket online Review, Critiphoria, Culver Chronicles, CURA, Curbside Splendor, Cyclamens and Swords, Cynic, Dandelion Farm Rev; Danse Macabre, Dark Matter, Dead Flowers, Dead Snakes, Decanto, decomP magazinE, Deimos eZine, Denver Syntax, Dialogist, Digital Papercut, Dislocate, District, Down in the Dirt, Dirty Chai, Dreams and Nightmares, Driftwood Press, Driftwood Review, Drunken Boat, EAB- Midnight Circus, EardrumPop, Earthborn, East Coast Ink, East Jasmine Review, Eat Your Words, Edge, Elsewhere Literary Magazine, EMG-zine, Empirical, Empty Sink Publishing, En Pointe Magazine, Entasis Journal, Entroper, Epigraph, Episodic, Eskimo Pie, Experimental Writing, Exquisite Corpse, Eunoia Review, Euphemism, Eureka, Every Day Poets, Exercise Bowler, Experiential-Experimental, Extraterrial Life, Extrac(s), Ezra, Fawlt Magazine, Fib Rev, Fiction Week Lit Review, Fictioneer, Fine Line, Fish Food & Lava Juice, Five Fishes Journal, Five Quarterly, Five Willow Literary Review, Flashquake, Flutter Poetry Journal, Flyover Country Review, Flywheel, Fogged Clarity, Folly, FoodFish Magazine, For Poetry, Four Ties Lit Rev, Fresh!, Foliate Oak, Forge, Fortunates, Foreign Encounters* (Anthology), *Fox Chase Review, FRiGG, Full of Crow, Furious Gazelle, Future Earth Mag, Gadfly, Gambling the Aisle, the Gap Toothed Madness, Gemini, the Germ, Gertrude Press, Gival Press LLC, Glass Seed, Gloom Cupboard, A Golden Place, Golden Sparrow Lit Rev, Gravel Magazine, Great American Poetry Show, Green Briar Review, Greensilk Journal, GUD, Gutter Eloquence Magazine, Haggard and Halloo, Hamilton Stone Review, Hando No Kuzushi, Hanging Moss Journal, Hazard Cat, Healthy Artist, HEArt, Heavy Hands Ink, Hermeneutic Chaos, Hermes Poetry Journal, High Coupe, Hobble Creek Review, Hobo Camp Review, HoboEye, Holly Rose Review, Honeyland Review, Horriefied Press* (suffer-anthology), *Horror Sleaze Trash, Hothouse Magazine, Houston Literary Journal, HOWL, Hungry Horrow, HyperText Magazine, the Ides of March, Ijagun Poetry Journal, Ikleftiko, Illya's Honey, Imitation Fruit Lit J, Indefinite Space, Indiana Voice, Inertia Magazine, Inner Art Journal, InQuire, Intercapillary Space, Iris Brown, Ishaan Lit Rev, IthacaLit, Lit Mag, Iron Bound, Jellyfish Whispers, Jersey Devil Press, Jesus Radicals, JMWW, Journal of Compressed Creative Art, Joyful!, Ken*again, Kill Poet, Kin, King Log, Konundrum Engine Literary Review, Kudzu, LA River of LA, Lamplit Underground, Lantern Review, Leaf Garden, Leaves of Ink, Legendary, Lies/Isle, Life As An, the Light Ekphrastic, Limn, Linden Avenue Lit Journal, Linnet's Wings, Liquid Imagination, Listenlight, Lit Chaos, Lit Up Mag, Literary Tonic, Literarily Erotic, Literary Mama, literary Orphans, Literary Underground, Literary Yard, Literati Quarterly, Loch Raven Review, Locust Magazine, A Long Story Short, Lost & Found, Lost Coast Review, Louiseville Review, Lummox, Mad Bunkers, Mad Hatters' Hat, Mad Swirl, Manhanttanville Rev, Marathon Literary Review, the Mas Tequila Review, McCroskey Memorial Internet Playhouse, Medullar Review, Magic Cat Press, Magic, Marco Polo, Mayo Review, Meadowland Review, MediaVirus, Meet for Tea, Mel Brake Press, Menopause Press, Midwest Lit Mag, Midway Journal, Miller's Pond, Miracle E.zine, Missing Slate, the Minetta Review, Milk, Milo Review, Miranda Literary Magazine, Misfit Magazine, Misfit's Miscellany, Mission at Tenth, Misty Mountain Review, Mixitini Matrix, Mojave River Review, Monongahela Review, Monterey*

*Poetry Review, Montucky Review, Moon City Review, Moon Magazine, Mosaic Art and Literary Jurnal, Mud Season Review, Muddy River Poetry Review, Muse, Mused, Mustard Seed Risk, Nain Rougue, Name Calling, A Narrow Fellow, the Natural Tale, The Nervous Breakdown, New Bourgeois, the New Writer, New York Dreaming, Noctua Review, Northwind, Nostrovia!Poetry, nthWORD, Obsession, Oddball Mag, Oddville Press, Offcourse , Off the Coast, Olentangy Review, On the Rusk, Open Window Review, Organs of Visions and Speech (OVS), Origami Poems, Orion Headless, Other Voices International Project, Otis Nebula, Outside in Literary and Travel Magazine, Outward Link, Over the Transom, Ozone Park Journal, Pagan Imagination, Paper Nautilus, Path, Peaches, Petrichor Machine, Poets Against War, PJ Nights, PANK, Past Simple, Paradise Review, the Pavillion, Pawnshop, Peeking Cat, Penhead Press, Pennsylvania Literary Journal, Peregrine Muse, Peripheral Surveys, Phantom Kangaroo, Picayune Review, Pink Chameleon, Pinstripe Fedora, Pirene's Fountain, Poem2Day, Poems-for-All, Poetry Quarterly, Poetry Repairs, Poetry Super Highway, Poets International, PoetsWest, Polu Texni, Poor Mojo's Alamanac(k), Poplorish, Poppy Road Review, Portmanteau, Post Script, Potomac: A Journal of Poetry and Politics, Poydras Review, Prairie Wolf Press Review, Praxilla, Press 1, PressBoard Press, Project Agent Orange Poetry Blog, Printer's Devil Review, Project Agent Orange Poetry, Prospective Journal [Cthullcu a love story-antholgoy], Protest Poems, Psychic Meatloaf, Purple Pig Literary Cup, Pyrokinection, Qrrtsiluni, Quatoble, Radar Poetry, Radioactive Moat, Radius, Rainbow Journal, Rampallian, Randomly Accessed Poetics, Raving Dove, Ray's Road Review, Red Booth Review, Red Box Kit, Red Dirt Review, Red Fez, Red Ochre Lit, Red River Review, Red Rose Review, Red Savina Review, Red Sky, Regime Books, Remarkable Doorway, Revolver, Rougarou, Right Hand Pointing, RiverLit, River Poets Journal, Roanoke Review, Rock Heals, Rock River Review, Rufous City Review, Rusty Nail, Sacred Ground Travel Magazine, Saint Elizabeth Street, Salt River Review, Sandy River Review, Sauced!, Sawbuck, Scapegoat Review, Scholars and Rogues, Scrambler, Scareship, Scissors and Spackles, Screaming Sheep, Scribblers and Inkspillers, Scene 4 , Scrubbadubdub, Sea Stories, See Spot Run, Sentinel Literary Quarterly, Shadowbox, Shampoo, Shelf Life, Shoot and Vines, Short, Fast & Deadly, Shot Glass, Shout Out, Shuf, Sick of Em, Silver Blade Poetry, Silver of Stone, Siren, Similar:Peaks::Poetry, Slate Literary Magazine, the Smoking Poet, SNM Horror Mag, Snow Monkey, SNReview, Songs of Erete Poetry Review, the Song Is, Soul to Soul, South 85, South Jersey Underground, Specs, Spectrum, Speculative Edge, Spinozablue, Spiral Orb, Spittoon, Spooky Boyfriend, Squalor Review, Squawk Back, Spry, St Somewhere, Star 82 Review, Stellar Showcase Journal, Step Away Magazine, Steel Toe Review, Stickman Review, Still Crazy, Stone Highway Review, Stone Path Review, Stonecoast Review, Stone's Throw, Storm Cycle (*Anthology*), Storyacious, Straight Forward: A Poetry Journal,Strange Machine, Stray Branch, Strong Verse, Subliminal Interiors, SubtleTea, Subtopian Mag, Sugared Water, Sundog Lit, Survivor's Review, Suss, Swamp Lily Review, Symmetry Pebbles, Syndic Literary Journal, Tawdry Bawdry, Telling Our Stories Press, THIS Literary Mag, This Zine Will Change Your Life, Thought Collection, Thought Smith, Tiferet, ongues of the Ocean, Tonopah Review, Torrid Literature, Tower Journal, trans lit mag, Treehouse, Triggerfish Critical Review, Trillium Literary Journal, Tule Review, Turk's Head Review, Turtle Island Quarterly, Turtle Way, Twisted Dreams, Two Hawks Quarterly, Typehouse Review, unFold, Unlikely 2.0, Untitled Country Review, Untitled with Passengers, Uprooted (anthology), Uptown Mosaic, Vagobond City Literary Journal, Verdad, Verse Wisconsin, Verseland, Versus Literary Journal, Viral Cat, Vis a Tergo, Visions with Voices, Voice Project, Volta, Vox Poetica, Waiting for the Bus, the Weary Blue, What's Your Sign (anthology), Wheelhouse Magazine, Whirlwind Review, Whistling Fire, White Ash Literary Magazine, Wild Violet, Wild Quarterly, Wilde Magazine, Wildness House Literary Review, Word Catalyst, Word Riot, Wordland, WORK Literary Magazine, Woven Tale Press, the Write Place at the Right Time, Write from Wrong, the Write Room, Write This, the Write Room, Writers' Bloc, Writer's Literary Muse, Writing Disorder, Yellow Mama, Yellow Medicine, Yes Poetry, Your Daily Poem, YoYo Magazine, Zodiac Review, Zona de Carga (loading zone), Zoomoozophone Review*
Zimbabwe: *Poetry Bulawayo*

In Chinese
Canada: *haiwaishikan* (*海外诗刊*)
China: *《世界诗人 》，《中国文学》(HK) ,《合澜海》*
Singapore: *《诗歌》《新华文学》*
US: changqingteng (*常青藤*), New World Poetry (print *新大陆诗刊*), *global times 《环球时报》*

Every time my work was accepted by one of the above, I felt more than delighted. Without such 'positive endorsement' from time to time, I would never have traveled thus far on a less trodden trail as an old Chinese village boy, who did not begin to learn the English alphabet in Shanghai as an ESL student until he was he was 19 years of age.

Yuan Changming
Vancouver, May 2015

About the Author

Yuan Changming, 8-time Pushcart nominee and author of four chapbooks, is the world's most widely published composer who speaks Mandarin but writes English. Growing up in a remote Chinese village, Yuan started to learn English at 19 and published several monographs on translation before moving to Canada. With a PhD in English from the University of Saskatchewan, Yuan currently co-edits *Poetry Pacific* with Allen Qing Yuan and runs Poetry Pacific Press in Vancouver. Since mid-2005, he has had poetry appearing in more than 1,000 literary journals/anthologies across 32 countries, which include *Asian Literary Review, Best Canadian Poetry* (2009, 2012, 2014), *Best New Poems Online, London Magazine, Paris/Atlantic, Poetry Kanto, SAND, Taj Mahal Review, Threepenny Review* and *Two Thirds North.*

www.ingramcontent.com/pod-product-compliance
Lightning Source LLC
LaVergne TN
LVHW051020080826
845145LV00009B/2711

* 9 7 8 0 9 7 8 7 9 7 5 6 0 *